SHALLOW

THE DEEP THOUGHT OF A MAD MAN

SONIA SO

ISBN 979-888521795-8

I thank my friends, they are the ones who suggested me towrite this story, I thank them. I thank my one friend, who helped in finding my grammar mistakes, I thank her. I thank my editor who edited this book and myself, for making this and the readers who are reading this, thank you all for supporting, I can't do this without you all.
Thank you all...

Contents

Foreword

My goal is to entertain you all, show my creativity by writing books. Many people like other types of stories but I like Thriller, suspicious, crime stories. There are many stories I think I didn't know how to show to people so, I wrote stories which I like! and I hope you like my stories.

Preface

I got the idea of writing this book was that... I and my friends were group chatting, that day I was upset for some reason, I told my friends that "I am very upset, please make me happy" Everyone tried everything to make me happy, suddenly, one of my friends, started role-playing as in her house, someone was there, we also joined and we made ourselves as FBI, murderer. Then, the co-author of this book, asked me if we can make a story, and we started to discuss it every day, and here it is! The final product. And also, the characters are also ourselves! Nyleone is me! and Rie is the co-author, the co-author's nickname was Rie, so she said that the character's name will be Rie. Kylie, Rose, Diana, Cherylynne were my friends, and we made them as characters

Acknowledgements

Message from the author: I want to thank who has helped in making my book! special thanks to the editor, she has helped me so much! she made all this for you. And again I want to thank them so much for helping me in making this book. Not to forget my viewers who read and view my books...

Prologue

Nyleone Sebastian, the main lead, lost her sisters and her father, she tried to find her sisters' murderer and knew that, the murderer actully works in the gang which her team/ FBI were finding. Will she able to find her sisters' murderer? Was murderer's intention was to kill Nyleone's sisters or someone told her to? To know more you have to read this story...

CHAPTER ONE

The greed of money

Hedwan was a peaceful city until it had gangsters, people were scared and didn't dare to go out but the Police and FBI (Federal Bureau of Investigation) will always make sure they are safe. The FBI is still finding who the gangsters are...

A normal woman was walking across a road, her name was Kylie Johann, she needed some money and was sad "I need some money... how will I get money? I am also not getting any jobs" she thought. Suddenly someone pulled her, he was a man wearing a black hoodie and a mask, Kylie got Startled and said, "W- who are you? leave me" she started shouting but the man shut her mouth with his and asked, "You want some money?" Kylie asked, "H- how did you know?" the man said in a husky voice, "I know everything," "How can I believe a stranger like you?" Kylie said, "You can trust me, I will give you the money" The man replied "Umm... Ok fine, but what should I do to get the money?" Kylie asked "You have to kill some people," The man said, "What? You want me to kill people?" Kylie asked, "Yes, you have to if you don't want to, then fine... " The man said

"Fine, I will do it. How much money will I get?" Kylie asked "You have to kill 3 people so one person it will be 10,000 Hed (Hedwan currency) so total, you will get

30,000 Hed. Do you accept this deal?" The man asked "Hmm... Ok, who are the 3 people?" Kylie asked, "Those three are siblings and their name is Sharon Sebastian, Nyleone Sebastian and, María Sebastian." The man said and showed her their photos, Kylie didn't ask why she has to kill them. "If you killed all the 3 sisters then I will give all the money, don't worry about the money, I will give you, you know your work so do it, here are my contacts, if anything happened then contact me," The man said and went away, Kylie also went away and thought to go her house, when she was going to her home, she saw someone, It was Nyleone! Kylie thought to kidnap and kill her, so she made a plan of how she will do that...

The plan was that: she would ask some questions and become friends with her. After that Kylie will take her to a place and there, she will kill her. All was going fine, Kylie started to go towards Nyleone and asked "Hi! I am Kylie, will you be my friend? Umm... I don't have any friends so I asked" Kylie said "Oh! I have met you the first time and I can't trust anyone here, sorry for the rejection, I don't want to be your friend" Nyleone said, hearing this Kylie was disappointed so she went away but, she hid behind a tree and started to watch Nyleone, she noticed Nyleone was messaging someone, and a few minutes later, she went inside a car... Kylie was near her house and took her scooter and started to chase Nyleone... after chasing her for so long, she finally overtook and came in front of her car and Nyleone had to stop her car, Kylie ran and caught Nyleone and punched her, Nyleone started to become unconscious, Kylie punched her more. Nyleone was unconscious, Kylie thought she was dead, but she couldn't throw the corpse in the road and run away... she saw a small hut near the road and thought to hide there, she hid it and went away.

She messaged the man, "I killed one of them. Where is my money?" but the man didn't reply. Kylie was also hungry, she knew some far-away restaurant so she went towards the restaurant with her scooter... after reaching the restaurant, she realized the restaurant was empty and only two people were there. They were, Sharon and María! Kylie acted like a normal customer and sat down in the chair, she took the tissue which was on the table and tried to pick up the knife with it, no one was watching her, and Kylie stabbed Sharon at the back and she instantly died, María, the restaurant owner saw it and tried to take a knife but before she could, Kylie stabbed her also. Sharon and María were dead. Suddenly a message came, "You killed the two sisters, what about the 3rd one? Here's your20,000 Hed. If you want more money then kill the 3rd sister also!" Seeing this, Kylie was shocked "The 3rd sister? Does he mean Nyleone? What? Nyleone is not dead? How? Whatever, I don't care if she is dead or not" Kylie said, "NO! You can't do that!" Nyleone saw everything, how her sisters died in front of her, Nyleone started to run away, Kylie chased her... somehow Nyleone escaped from Kylie. She started to cry... she went to her office, the FBI office.

Yes, Nyleone is an FBI agent and their mission was to find the gangster, Nyleone thinks Kylie is one of the members of gangsters and has to be prisoned her. They started to find her... Nyleone met her good friend Rie Bach, she told her everything that happened with her and in María's restaurant. Rie felt sad for her "May Sharon and María rest in peace" she said. Some officers went to María's restaurant for the investigation...

CHAPTER TWO

Wanted Criminal: Kylie Johann

Some officers took Sharon and María to bury them. Nyleone was crying and couldn't see her sisters like this. She sat near a rock and thought... What could be that woman's name?" Rie came and asked her "What are you thinking?" "The woman who killed my sisters, her name is Kylie, but I don't know her full name..." Nyleone said "Don't worry about that, we will find her" Rie said. Other FBI officers went to see some evidence, in many places, bloodstains were there, they found a knife on the ground, so they picked it and went to the office, for investigation. Others analyzed the restaurant. The officers went to the FBI office and started to investigate, they thought to find some fingerprints but they couldn't find any fingerprints because Kylie had picked the knife when she had tissues in her hand, so her fingerprints didn't come in the knife. All thought to call Nyleone because she had seen the murderer's face. They called Nyleone, "Officer Nyleone, you have seen the murderer's face?" They asked "Yes! And her name is Kylie" "We have called an artist. If you tell her how she looks, then we can find her" The officers said "Sure! I will tell" and Nyleone started to describe how Kylie looks, the artist was drawing it, at last, they got how Kylie looks... They took the drawing of Kylie and started to put it everywhere in the city as she is the wanted criminal. They asked everyone if they saw or knew her but no one had seen her.

Meanwhile, Kylie was scared and messaged the man "Everyone in the Hedwan is finding me, help me!" A few minutes later, a message came, it was an address and another message was, "Come to this place". Kylie went there, when she reached there, she saw the man and went near him, "Why do you want to kill those three sisters?" she asked but the man didn't reply, "Why couldn't you kill Nyleone?" He asked "I don't know! I punched her till death but... How? Did she pretended to be dead?" Kylie asked.

Okay, I will tell you what happened to her, she was not dead, you just made her unconscious, but how did she not die by getting beaten up, even I don't know" The man said, "What is your name?" Kylie asked "What? What you are gonna do if you knew my name?" The man asked, "I mean, I don't know your name, so how can I call you?" Kylie asked "You can call me Mr. Dean," Dean said "Okay, Mr. Dean," Kylie said "Now silently come with me," Dean said, Kylie nodded and they walked until they reach their destination, Kylie saw 2 tall buildings, "From now on, you will stay here only, come with me to building 1," Dean said "Okay" Kylie replied, they entered Building 1, it was a very huge, many people were there, they were roaming around, while others, they were doing their business. Then, Dean called a woman who was passing by, "Listen, she is new here, so show her around," he said, the woman nodded and asked "Hello! What is your name?" "My name is Kylie Johann" Kylie replied, "My name is Cherylynne

Parks, Nice to meet you. I think Boss have told you that you will work and stay here" Cherylynne said, "Boss? Do you mean Mr. Dean?" Kylie asked, Cherylynne nodded, "So this is building 1, where all our members work, it is nothing but an office, it has 5 floors," Cherylyne said. "And here, you will also work. Now what you will work on, I will tell you later or Tomorrow when Boss will say something. Now come with me into building 2" Cherylynne said, they went to building 2. They saw, a cafeteria so Kylie asked "What is this? Is this is a cafeteria?" "Yes, here you can eat, breakfast, lunch, snacks, and dinner. Now, what is the timing for it, you can ask the Aunt, right there" Cherylyne pointed towards the aunt, "And this also has 5 floors, in this building all the members stay here, and you will also stay, each floor contains 400 rooms so total, 20,000 rooms. On the ground floor, the cafeteria and all other floors have rooms to stay. I think your room number would be near 1050. You can ask about this to the woman at the counter, right there" Cherylyne said and pointed to the counter. "If you want anything then you can ask me, my room number is 343," Cherylyne said, "Will you be my friend?" Kylie asked, "What?" Cherylynne asked, "I don't have any friends here, a-and I know only you here" Kylie said "Okay, I will be your friend," Cherylynne said, "Thank you," Kylie said "Okay, I have to do work, so bye," Cherylynne said and went away. Kylie went towards the counter and asked the woman, the receptionist... "Hey, I am new... member here! So I need my room keys" Kylie asked, "Okay mam, can you tell me your name? I have to ask it with Boss also" The receptionist asked, "It Is Kylie Johann" Kylie said "Okay, your room number is 1051, and here are the keys, your room is on the 2nd floor" The receptionist said, Kylie took her keys and went towards the cafeteria ...

"Aunt, can you tell the timing for the food?" Kylie asked, "Breakfast- 7 to 9 AM, Lunch- 11 to 1 PM, Snacks- 4 to 6 PM, and Dinner- 7 - 9 PM," The aunt said... Kylie thanked her and went to her room.

CHAPTER THREE

The Truth and the first mission of Kylie

Kylie sat in the bed and thought something, "Whatever I did, was it right? Of course, it is not! But... Why did I do that? If I just sleep for a moment then, I should not think about these things!" soon Kylie fell asleep. After a few hours, someone knocked at Kylie's door. It was Cherylynne! Kylie woke up and opened the door, "What happened, Cherylynne?" Kylie asked, "Nothing happened, As now it is 4 PM so I came to call you for the snacks... Do you wanna eat some snacks?" Cherylynne asked, "Ya sure! But first, let me wash my face then I will come" Kylie said and went to the bathroom, Cherylynne was waiting for her. After Kylie washed her face, they went to the cafeteria. They took their snacks and sat in, "The pancakes are looking very delicious!" Kylie said Cherylynne agreed with it, "I want to ask you something!" Kylie said, "What do you want to ask?" Cherylynne said, "Why are these people here?" Kylie asked, "Don't you know? These people are members of the gang, the gang which the FBI of Hedwan is finding! And I, you, everyone are the members of this gang! But do you know what is the name of our gang? **Skull soul**!" Cherylynne said Kylie was shocked after hearing it

"I was in the gang but still... I didn't realize it" Kylie said, "I think Boss didn't tell you about this" Cherylynne said, "What can I even do? I am already in this group! But... I am here because I am a criminal and so Boss brought me here, what did they do that they are here? Are they criminals like me? And you also?" Kylie asked, "Maybe some of us are criminals, and to be safe they are here. But, most of us are here for money, and even I, I am also doing for money" Cherylynne said, "What? Why are these people harming Hedwan? Are they also from Hedwan?" Kylie asked, "Some of them are from Hedwan but most of them are from other states and countries!" Cherylynne said. Kylie and Cherylynne ate their snacks and went to their room, Kylie felt very depressed so she slept...

The next day, it was 5 in the morning, and Cherylynne knocked at Kylie's door, Kylie woke up and said "What happened? Why did you come at this time? I think it's 5 AM" "Sorry for the disturbance, Boss has given us a mission in which you are also involved! So, I have come here to call you, be ready and come to the office by 5:40 AM" Cherylynne said and went away... Kylie washed her face and brushed, after taking a bath she went to Building 1. On the ground floor of Building 1, she met Cherylynne and they went to the 2nd Floor. They met Willam Jordan, "Hello I am Willam Jordan, as Boss has given us a mission which includes; I, Cherylynne Parks, Kylie Johann, Serena woods, and Stanley Woolf," Willam said, "So, the mission is that we have to kidnap a woman named Nyleone Sebastian" Willam showed everyone Nyleone's picture, "I think Kylie tried to kill Nyleone, but here, we don't have to do that, just kidnap her. Kylie will be in danger if she went freely, I don't know why Boss has ordered to bring Kylie also, she is a criminal there, so anyone can identify her, we have to make a plan!"

Willam said "Kylie can hide her face, wearing a mask, hat, and sunglasses and not go out from the vehicle," Serena said "Yes, we can do that, and she can guide us from the vehicle," Stanley said "Okay fine. From here to Hedwan it will take 1 hour because we will go from a secret path as directly we can't go, it can be dangerous" Willam said, they went outside of building 1, they sat in Willam's car and went towards Hedwan by a secret path...

CHAPTER FOUR

The Mission: Kidnap Nyleone

After 1 hour, they reached Hedwan. But, A cop stopped them, "Do you know this woman? Have you seen her?" It was Kylie! But, they said "No, we don't know her and we didn't see her" "Oh, Okay, you can go," The cop said, but when he saw Kylie in disguised, he got suspicious but he ignored it. After a few minutes, "Don't go anywhere" Willam said to Kylie, "We are going to Nyleone's house because she's in there, Kylie you can go to one of our crew's house" Cherylynne said, she took Kylie to someone's house and knocked the door, someone came, it was Diana Curie, "You will stay in her house and guide us, take this camera, we will also have a camera, this both cameras are connected, by seeing this camera, you can see and guide us, we will call you when we will reach Nyleone's house so you can guide us, and if you are in any danger then seek help from Diana, we are going to Nyleone's house, bye" Cherylynne said and went away with others. "Hi, so you are a member of Skull soul?" Kylie asked Diana "Yes, I am the spy in the gang, and I live here. I also work in the FBI and give information to the office," Diana said, "FBI? You mean where Nyleone works?" Kylie asked, "Yes," Diana said. "Have you ever thought, whatever you are doing is it correct? Like you are working in a gang!" Kylie asked, "What? That's a random question" Diana said, "You know... I am a cri- criminal..., don't you feel weird and stressful" Kylie asked. Kylie was asking this type of question because she was already stressed. "No. I was not stressed or anything, I even think I don't have emotions, anything bad happens then I will not cry, anything good happens, I will not laugh. Am I emotionless??" Diana said..."At first, when I was newly a spy, I always thought that I was destroying a city. I always thought what do Hedwan's citizens feel that in their city, spies are roaming and stealing all information. Let's forget it, I don't wanna talk about this" Diana said, "Yeah, I also thought like this" Kylie said, a few moments later, Cherylynne called Kylie, " We reached Nyleone's house" Cherylynne said, "Do you have the medicine which will make people unconscious?" Kylie asked, "Yes, we have. What should we do," Cherylynne asked, "Okay, I know where Nyleone is, she is in her bedroom, doing something on her laptop," Willam said, "Umm... oh I see! There is a window next to her bedroom, Cherylynne and Serena can come to the bedroom by the window, they will try to catch Nyleone, if they will be in trouble then Willam and Stanley will come from the door and help them, do you understand the plan?" Kylie said, "Yes, we understood," all said. As the plan, Cherylynne and Serena went near the window, and by the window, they came inside the room and tried to catch Nyleone but, Nyleone had her gun but before she could shoot it, Willam came and unconscious Nyleone. "That was very close!" Stanley said, "Thank goodness, that she didn't shoot the bullets, otherwise it will make noise and the cops would come," Kylie said, "We have to take Nyleone to our building or headquarters, but we can't take her like this, we have to hide her face, body..." Serena said, "Yes, Serena is right, see in her closet, if there is any cloth", so Serena went and saw inside the closet, there were some clothes so they took them and from that, they hide Nyleone's face and body. They took her in their car and went towards Diana's house, and Kylie also came in the car. They went towards their Headquarters. "What do we do next? We completed this mission," Stanley asked, "Boss hasn't told yet, what is the next mission but I think he will say when we will reach our Headquarters" Cherylynne said...

CHAPTER FIVE

Torture with Nyleone

They reached their headquarter, Cherylynne got a message from the Boss, "Go back 5 meters of building 2", they went back and saw a hole, in the hole there were stairs, "Do we have to go in there? In that hole?" Serena asked, "I think yes," Willam said, "Okay, then let's go," Kylie said, they went downstairs, when they reached the end of the stairs, they saw a big hall, there was also a big box made of glass, filled with water. All were surprised, "What is this place!?" Stanley asked, there was a chair, the boss sent another message, "Make Nyleone sit in the chair" Cherylyne said aloud the Boss's message, Serena and kylie placed Nyelone on the chair. The next message came from the Boss, "Take a rest now, after taking rest, if you go little far away in the West direction, you will see a dark-colored ladder, take that ladder near the glass box, place it, and then take Nyeleone and tie her leg with the chain in the top of the box. Once you have done all of this, I will tell you what to do next.," Cherylynne said aloud the Boss's message, "What!? We will torture Nyleone? didn't think that!" Stanley said, "Okay, let's take a rest for now..." Willam said. After a few minutes, "Okay I am going to bring the ladder, so where do I have to go?" Willam asked, Kylie, pointed at the west and Willam went towards that direction. After a few minutes, Willam came with the ladder and placed it near the box, "Now, someone has to take Nyleone, who will do that?" Willam asked, "Me and Kylie?" Cherylynne said, "Okay," Kylie said. Serena was holding the ladder. They took Nyleone and tied her leg with the chain, Nyleone was hanging... "Now what to do?" Stanley asked, "Okay, oh Boss has sent a message, 'Now bring water from the building,'" Cherylynne said, so Stanley went to bring water, soon Stanley came with a water bucket. "Now pour that water in Nyleone's face so that she would wake up," Cherylynne read the message, Stanley climbed the ladder, poured the water on Nyleone's face and she woke up, "WHERE I AM!? WHY I AM SEEING UPSIDE-DOWN!?" Nyleone shouted, "Hey! What is the next task!?" Stanley asked, "Come down! I want to say something to Nyleone!" Willam said Stanley came down and Willam went up, "So, Nyleone, you are nowhere but in Skull Soul's base," Willam said to Nyleone, "WHAT!!?? I am kidnapped by the wanted gang!! WHY??" Nyleone asked, "Even we don't know, hah hah," Willam replied, "Willam stop chatting with her," Cherylynne said, "Boss's next message is that, 'Now all can go to the building, your mission is finished'. So let's go!" Cherylynne said, "What about Nyleone? She will just hang here?" Stanley asked, 'I think yes" Cherylynne said, so all went towards the stairs, "HEY! HEY! LET ME GET DOWN, DON'T LEAVE ME HERE!!" Nyleone was shouting but everyone ignored her, they left Nyleone alone. A few minutes later, someone came, "Who are you?" Nyleone asked, "Mr. Dean" Dean replied, "Dean?" Nyleone asked, Dean, climbed the stairs, and said to Nyleone, "I am the boss of Soul Skull! Your FBI team is finding me, right?" Dean asked, "What!? So you are the Boss! Killing people in Hedwan! Why?" Nyleone asked, "Stop questioning! I will do you a favor" Dean said,

"Favor? What is the favor?" Nyleone asked, "I will untie your legs and wouldn't drop you in the water, you can go back to Hedwan safely, but you have to join Skull Soul! And you can also spy on the FBI, so what do you think? Your life or your job?" Dean asked, "I will never join this gang!" Nyleone said, "Fine!" Dean replied, Dean, climbed down and went a little far away, and came back with a big lever, and placed on the floor, "If you don't want to, then enjoy this torture!" Dean said, Dean, pulled the lever and Nyleone fell in the water, again Dean pulled the lever and Nyleone came out of the water. Dean again did, Nyleone again fell, and again came out. This happened for a few minutes, Dean was tired from this, "I think you are enjoying this torture, BUT I DON'T!! Hang here only! And also, when I will leave this hall, this hall will completely become very cold, the temperature would be probably -10℃ " Dean said, Dean started to walk towards the stairs and left the hall, the hall started to become cold.

CHAPTER SIX

Nyleone is kidnapped

In the FBI office, Hedwan. Rie was investigating, suddenly, she thought, "Where is Nyleone? Today she didn't even come! It's been noon! Don't know where she is... hmm..." Then she told the crew, "I am going to find Nyleone! I am having a feeling that she is in danger!" Rie said and went to Nyleone's house, but she found out that, Nyleone was not in her house, but when she went to see her bedroom, she saw that the closets were not closed, some clothes were fallen out from the closet, she saw Nyleone's gun, which was in the floor. Rie couldn't understand anything, so she thought to go back to the office, but she saw some footprints in the doorway, "Okay! Now I understood! Someone came to Nyleone's house and then kidnapped her? By looking at the footprints, maybe there were 3-5 people, and 2 footprints are leading to... the bedroom's window! I am 100% sure! Some people have kidnapped Nyleone!" Rie rushed to the FBI Office, "Nyleone is kidnapped! We have to find her! Does anybody know who it can be? Ask everyone in Hedwan about Nyleone!" Rie was asking people about Nyleone, Rie had a picture of Nyleone, seeing that picture, a girl came near Rie and said, "Are you finding this woman?" "Yes! Have you seen her?" "Is her house in 13th Street?" The girl asked, "Umm... Yes, but how do you know?" Rie asked, "I am her sister's friend, I went to her house," The girl said, "Oh! Friend of Sharon... So, have you seen her?" Rie asked again, "I saw some people, in their car, taking a person, covered with clothes, and they were going out from sister Nyleone's house!" The girl said, "Covered with clothes... in Nyleone's closet, the clothes were fallen, the footprints... the people" Rie thought, "H-how many people were there in the car?" Rie asked, "5 people," The girl said, "AS I thought 3-5 people, they were 5!" Rie thought, "What is your name?" Rie asked, "Rose Luther," the girl said, "Thank you so much, Rose! I will never forget your help, again, Thank you!" Rie said, Rose, smiled. Rie went to the FBI office and said everyone that Nyleone is kidnapped, "I got a footage near Nyleone's house, and maybe they are the people" A crew member said, "Wait a minute, I will show this footage to the Girl" Rie said and went outside to find Rose, after finding her, Rie asked, "Did these people went out from Nyleone's house?" "Yes!" Rose replied, "Thank you.." Rie said and went back to the FBI office, "Okay, these people only kidnapped Nyleone! Find the car number!" Rie said, "The number is not visible but... if I look closely, it is TJ 20 WG 4038, and the owner is Willam Jordon!" "Does Willam live in Hedwan?" Rie asked, "No," A crew member said, "See more footage of that car! They have left Hedwan, but where? Find that, I will try to find more information about this!" Rie said, she asked everyone that 'have they seen this car going somewhere?'. But no one knows, after a few hours, Rie went to the FBI office, "Any luck? Have you got any information, have you got any footage?" Rie asked in a tired voice, "Only one!" The crew member said, "But let's take a little break, I am tired," The crew member said, "Sure!" Rie said, a few minutes later, "Okay Agent Rie, this is the footage I got!" And the crew member showed the footage, it was near the gate of Hedwan. Suddenly, he found something, "I also found another footage! See this! It is 34th Street! They first went to the gate then they went to 34th street! Look at the time, in the gate- 10: 03 AM, and in the 34th Street- 10:08 AM" The crew said, "And 34th Street has only one path leading to North! They went there only!" Rie said, "So let's go there! We will go to the North! Then maybe we can find Nyleone, and also... why I do feel like the gang iis doing this" Rie said.

CHAPTER SEVEN

Let's rescue Nyleone and Raid Skull Soul!

Rie and the Crew went towards the North of 34th street by car. "Will there be any turns on this road?" Rie asked, "I think no! There are no turns" The crew member said, after going in a straight way for 1 hour, they reached the end... "So, we have reached?" Rie asked, "There is nothing! It's just Forest!" The crew member said, "Let's cross this Forest" Rie said in a serious tone, "What? You think there is something behind this Forest!?" The Crew member said, "Yes!" Rie replied, "Fine! Let's go" The crew member said, they tried to cross the forest but, because of bushes, and vines, they were unable to go but somehow they managed to get out, suddenly, they saw something, they saw Skull Soul's headquarters, it was just 30 meters away, after going 30 meters ahead, they saw the headquarter, they were shocked, Rie was seeing here and there, she noticed a woman was there near the trees, so Rie and the Crew went near her, they noticed that it was Nyleone! Rie was happy and hugged Nyleone, they took Nyleone to their car without noticing by the Skull Soul, "Nyleone what happened? Why you were near Skull Soul's base?" Rie asked, suddenly, someone shot bullets, Rie and Nyleone tried to hide in the car, but the crew which came with Rie got the shots, "No!" Rie said, The crew were dead on the spot, Rie and Nyleone were shocked. They took their car and went towards Hedwan before the shooter shoots them. "What happened to you? How were you there in Skull Soul's base?" Rie again asked, "I was kidnapped by them in the morning, they took me to a hall, there, they hanged me with a chain, at the top of a big box filled with water! After some minutes, I met the boss of their gang! He told himself as 'Mr. Dean'. He offered me to join the Gang. But, I denied it, and because of that, he tortured me! Dived me into that big box filled with water, he also told me that, when he leaves the hall, the hall will become very cold!" Nyleone said, "If the hall was cold, you would have died, right? How are you alive?" Rie asked, "Listen to the whole story, it was just 5 minutes, I was somehow alive in the cold hall, suddenly, the hall stopped being cold and, Kylie came to see me, and said me 'Whatever I did to your sisters, I am really sorry... I didn't have any intentions for it. I know you will die here, but, if somehow you survived, then, can you do me a favor? please kill me...' I was listening all the time, she went towards the stairs and went away but, the hall stopped being cold! Then I untied myself from the chain, I fell in the water, went outside of the box by the ladder, I went out of the hall and stayed near the forest. I knew you would come, so I waited... When I came out of the hole, it was just 4 PM!" Nyleone said, "But how did you know that it was... 4 PM?" Rie asked, "By seeing the Sun," Nyleone said, "Oh!" Rie replied, "Then I waited for some minutes, then you and your mates came to rescue me!" Nyleone said, "But... sadly they died," Rie said in a sad tone, "Now we have found Skull Soul's Headquarters, The FBI can easily raid it!" Nyleone said, "Yes, we will raid them!"

Rie said, and they both went towards Hedwan. By 6 PM, they reached Hedwan and told everyone that, "We found the gang's Headquarters! The Skull Soul's Headquarters!" Rie said, "Oh! That's a great thing to hear, we will raid it and arrest them!! They have killed many of Hedwan's citizens..."said the seniors of Rie and Nyleone, "Yes sir!" said Nyleone. The next day, at 7 AM, they went to Skull Soul's Headquarters but they found out that there was no one! Everything was empty, there was nothing in the rooms. Rie and Nyleone were shocked, "You told me this is their headquarters, then where are they?!" The senior asked in an angry voice. "Sir, we don't know. Yesterday, we saw! They were here but... today they are not, they went somewhere... I think" Nyleone said, Now let's go back to Hedwan, if you get any clue about Skull Soul, then first confirm it and then tell us!" The senior said, "Yes sir!" Rie and Nyleone said. And they went back to Hedwan, disappointed. But, the Skull Soul went somewhere else. They went 20 kilometers away from their old headquarters, they found 2 new buildings, the building 1, as their new office with 5 floors and building 2, for their living with 231 floors... Yesterday at 4 PM, Mr. Dean knew that Nyleone escaped the Hall, he knew that Nyleone will somehow escape and go back to Hedwan, so he tried to find some buildings to live and work in, he found the 2 buildings in Jeksoda and bought them. first, his gang lived in Losia Medran Forest, and now, shifted to Jeksoda. (Skull Soul's new headquarters) Willam called everyone, "So, we all know that I, Kylie, Cherylynne, Serena, and Stanley went to kidnap Nyleone, we put her in the hole which is 2 meters away from our buildings, anyone knows how Nyleone escaped the Hole?" Willam asked, Kylie, started to become nervous, "Oh no! I think I forgot to close the door and so,

Nyleone escaped?" Kylie thought.

CHAPTER EIGHT

The bitter old days (Rie's backstory)

The next day, Rie and Nyleone were talking about the incident that happened yesterday, suddenly Nyleone felt thirsty so she told Rie, "Rie! Can you bring water from the canteen". The chef of the Canteen was very strict and no one dare to go near the canteen, Nyleone wanted Rie to get scolded, just for fun, even though she knew the Chef is very strict, so she asked. "Sorry, but I will not go" Rie replied, "Hah hah! You are scared, right?" Nyleone teased, "No! I am not scared by the Chef!" Rie said, suddenly, something came up in Rie's mind. "Nyleone, we have known each other for the past 7 years but... you don't know many things about me! My Childhood!" Rie said, "What are you talking about, Rie?" Nyleone asked, "Do you know my father's name?" Rie asked, "Yes! It's Benjamin Bach," Nyleone said, "But... he was not my real father!" Rie said, "What!?" Nyleone was shocked, "Now, I will tell you my heartbroken childhood..." Rie started to narrate her backstory, "My real name is Rie Shelley, at 2007, when I was 7-years-old, my mother became sick, we called many doctors, tried many medicines but, we were not able to cure her. After 3 months later, unfortunately, my mother died. Because of this, I and father were very sad, and my father also started to drink alcohol, he always came late home with some alcohol bottles and always loses his sense. "Father! You are going the wrong way!" I say, "SHUT UP!" He says and pushes me, I would sometimes, cry. It became my routine, wait for father, and then get beaten by him! Yes, every day, he loses his sense and then beats me. I suffered this pain and kept quiet until I was 10-year-old, I saw a hammer, I decided to throw that hammer on my father to get rid of him!

When he came back home, I threw the hammer into my father's head, he fell on the floor. I didn't panic, I didn't scream but I ran away from the home. I lived in Mikin, from Mikin, I came to Hedwan, I didn't know what to do, as I didn't have any money, I thought to tell the police about this, so I looked for the police station, after finding it, I told the police officers about it, "She is an orphan, we should take her to the orphanage!" They said to themselves, suddenly, a police officer saw me, he asked me, "Who are you, child? What happened to you?" His friends told him about my problem, he became happy and said to me, "Child, I and my wife, don't have any children. So, can we adopt you? I promise, we will take care of you and be a good parent" He said, " I didn't know what to do, so I replied, "Sure! You can adopt me!" I thought, 'this is a chance of being happy again, but with new parents'. And the Police officer who adopted me was Benjamin Bach. I went to his house, met his wife, and told her what happened to me for the past 3 years. I changed my surname to Bach, and we three lived a happy life, but... with my real mother and father also, I lived a happy life for 6 and a half years..." Rie completed her narration, hearing this, "You have suffered so much in childhood, I thought you are Coward! But you have already felt the scariest things, your father beating you... any child would have screamed... I am ashamed of myself, who thought you would get scolded by the chef. I am sorry!" Nyleone apologized, "It's okay! Getting scolded by the chef... hmmm, but did you know that the chef has already transferred!" Rie said, "What!?" Nyleone was surprised, Rie started to laugh, "Why didn't you tell me! I always thought, when will we get rid of him!" Nyleone said. Nyleone and Rie started to laugh.

CHAPTER NINE

The betrayal

The next day, Cherylynne and Diana were on a call, Cherylynne informed Diana that they shifted to a new place, "Yes, we have shifted to Jeksoda! Have you told this to Aiden?" Cherylynne asked, "Aiden?" Diana asked, "Yes, Aiden Schumacher! He is also a spy from Skull Soul like you, don't you remember him?" Cherylynne asked, "Aiden Schumacher... Oh yeah! For a few days he was not in contact with me, today I will tell him about this," Diana said, "Okay" Cerylynne said and she hang up the call. Diana called Aiden, "Hello?" Diana said, "Hello, what happened Diana?" Aiden asked, "I have to say something about Skull Soul!" Diana said, "Oh, but I don't have time now, can we talk in person?" Aiden asked, "Sure, can we meet at 2 PM, at the 2nd Street, today?" Diana asked, "Okay" Aiden replied, at 2 PM they met at the 2nd Street, "So Diana what you wanted to say?" Aiden asked, "Yes, I wanted to say that, Skull Soul has shifted to Jeksoda! Today Cherylynne told me about this, as Nyleone had found Skull Soul's previous location" Diana said, "Diana... For how many months have you stayed here?" Aiden asked, "What? That's a very strange question... I lived here, nearly a year" Diana replied, "You also know that you are a spy of the Skull Soul, right?" Aiden asked, "Yes, I know that I am a spy! Why are you asking this type of question?" Diana was confused, "Because you are a fool!" Aiden said, hearing this, Diana was shocked, she started to feel that she is betrayed. Suddenly someone grabbed her, it was the FBI! Diana started to scream, "AIDEN!! AIDEN!! WHY ARE FBI'S HERE!??" Diana was screaming but Aiden was doing nothing, Diana realized that she was betrayed, and started to cry...

Aiden Schumacher, was a spy from Skull Soul, as Diana and Aiden were the first 2 spies of Skull Soul, they started to work together. Nothing big happens, that's why only 2 spies were there. Diana and Aiden also became very good friends and always trusted each other. But when the FBI found out about Skull Soul, Aiden stopped talking to Diana, and they both started to forget each other... The reason why Aiden stopped talking to Diana was...

2 months ago, the FBI found him, "So you worked for Skull Soul and were spying on us!?" The FBI asked. Aiden told everything about himself that he is a spy from Skull Soul to save himself but didn't tell anything about Skull Soul, "Do you have any partner with you?" The FBI asked, Aiden was surprised, he didn't want Diana to get caught, so he lied... "No, I don't have any partner!" Aiden said, The FBI also gave him an offer, if you want to save yourself then, you have to help the FBI and spy on the Skull Soul, if you agree with this offer then we will not prison you for working in a gang. Aiden agreed to that deal and betrayed Skull Soul. 2 months later, the FBI knew that Aiden had a partner, "Do you know who Diana Curie is?" The FBI asked, Aiden didn't say anything, "We also knew that she is your partner!" The FBI said Aiden was surprised, "We don't know where she is, that's why you will find her if you didn't then we will kill her! We knew you are here to save her" The FBI said, and hearing this, he was shocked,

suddenly a call came, "Hello?" Diana said... Aiden fooled her and brought her to 2nd street, he knew Diana would say 2nd Street as no one lives there... he went there with the FBI and the FBI caught her, Aiden couldn't do anything but, only can see the situation, "I am sorry Diana! I was just trying to save you... But I failed. Hope nothing bad happens to you" Aiden thought. Diana was taken to the prison, a few minutes later, Aiden came to see her, "You... You betrayed me!" Diana said, "No!" Aiden said and told the whole story that he wanted to save her... "Diana started to cry, "I am sorry...", "please don't cry," Aiden said, "I am not crying because you betrayed the whole Skull Soul, and me? This is the tears of joy, I am very lucky to have such a good friend!" Diana said and smiled, "You will be in jail for 5 years?" Aiden asked, "Yes!" Diana said, "Well, I have a surprise for you!" Aiden said, "What is the surprise?" Diana asked, "I will tell when everything gets over! This Skull Soul, the gang... after all this problem gets over, I will tell you!" Aiden said, "Okay," Diana said and gave a gentle smile. Aiden went away.

CHAPTER TEN

FBI found the Skull Soul's new base

Aiden went to the FBI office and was told: "I have found Skull Soul's new base, It is Jeksoda!" "Do we directly go there and raid it?" A crew member asked, "No... They can easily know" Rie said, "Then what should we do? How can we catch them?" The crew asked, "They would be probably more than 1000, we can't catch all of them! Can they all die for good?" Nyleone asked, "What?!?" Everyone was confused, "I have a plan, can we put bombs in their headquarters? Because of that, the building will collapse and all will die for good" Nyleone said, "Yes! They have killed many civilians of Hedwan, they should be punished! We can't just prison all of them" Rie said, Everyone thought for a moment... "Okay, fine, we will do that!.

They got permission from higher-ups to kill the gang.

We will plant bombs in their building, but how will we do that?" The FBI said, "We will send Aiden to plant the bombs, as he is also a member of the gang" Nyleone said, "Okay" They agreed. Rie, Aiden took the bombs and went to Jeksoda, they saw two tall buildings, "Is this the new base of Skull Soul?" Rie asked, "Yes, before going, Diana told, the tall white buildings are the base of Skull Soul," Aiden said, "Okay, now go to the building and plant the bombs!" Rie said, "No, I can't go, they check if the person came has the Skull Soul Badge!" Aiden said, "What? Badge?" Rie was confused, "Yes, that's why I brought it," Aiden said, and wore the badge... and went towards the building. The security checked Aiden, "Oh! You have the badge, okay you can go, but... what is this bag?" The security looked at the bag (which was filled with bombs), "Oh, it's nothing, just my clothes, I have come here to live, at first, I lived at Hedwan because I was a spy..." Aiden started to narrate his story, Rie took a stick and smashed it in the securities' head, and they became unconscious, "Yes! Our plan worked!" Aiden said. They had the plan that Aiden will distract the securities and Rie will smash a stick onto their head so that they will become unconscious... Aiden went inside the building, and Rie took securities' bodies to hide somewhere, after hiding, she waited for Aiden. Aiden started to plant bombs without noticing... after planting enough bombs, he went outside the building. Aiden and Rie went a little far away, Rie took the remote from which they will blow up Skull Soul's base... Rie pressed the button, and the building blew up! The building started to collapse, "AAAGHH!!! WHAT IS HAPPENING!!!??" in the building all were shouting, but not Kylie... "Nyleone? you have done it! you have done my favor! I can't believe... I can't believe it... Thank... you... Ny-Nyleone" Kylie thought, and everyone died. A few minutes later, the FBI came, "Kylie... Did she also die?" Nyleone asked, "Yes, I think," Rie said, "Guess, her favor is done!" Nyleone said, "We have to find the Boss! We have to catch him, if we didn't then he would bring more people!" Aiden said, "All started to find Mr. Dean, suddenly they saw a man, Rie went near him and asked, "Have you seen this guy?" and showed a picture of

Mr. Dean, "It's me..." The man said, all looked at him, Mr. Dean always wore a mask, but this time, he showed his read face to everyone, the FBI caught him, "Yes! He is boss, his voice and face shape, it is all similar..." Aiden said, "I surrender myself! I knew my building has collapsed and got destroyed, and my gang members have also died! I can't do anything alone, that's why I am surrendering myself!" Mr. Dean said. The FBI took Mr. Dean to Hedwan Prison, Mr. Dean was sentenced to prison forever! Mr. Dean will be forever in Prison...

CHAPTER ELEVEN

All were in the Hedwan and were happy, "Now Hedwan can live peacefully again!" Rie said, "Yes! Finally, we caught the boss! Tomorrow, the FBI is gonna ask questions to Mr. Dean, right?" Nyleone asked, "Yes! They will ask him 'why did he start a gang?' 'What was his intention' and ask some personal questions" Rie said, "Oh..." Nyleone replied. They saw Aiden, "Aiden! Where are you going?" Rie asked, "Nowhere," Aiden said and started to blush, "Why are you blushing?" Nyleone asked, "I am going to meet Diana, bye!" Aiden said and went away, "Is that a thing to get shy? He could just say it normally" Rie asked, "Don't know," Nyleone said, Aiden went to Hedwan Prison and met Diana, "Diana! It's me!" Aiden said in a joyful voice, "Oh... Aiden, The situation is over? Skull Soul got arrested?" Diana asked, Aiden told her everything about what happened to Skull Soul's Building and Mr. Dean. "Diana, I have come here to tell you something," Aiden said, "Oh yes!" Diana replied, "The FBI has given Bail to you!" Aiden said, "What!? Really!?" Diana said, "Yes because I helped them a lot in the finding of Skull Soul, they gave bail to you... Now we can live together!" Aiden said, The policeman came and opened Diana's cell door, Diana hugged Aiden and they went out of the prison. Aiden and Diana started to live together, and became best friends...

The next day, Nyleone went to Rie's house, "Hello Rie! I need your help," Nyleone said, Nyleone went inside and sat in the chair, "What happened?" Rie asked, "Do you know Kylie?" Nyleone asked, "Yes! I know, why? What happened?" Rie replied, "One day, she told me, 'please kill me, why would someone want to die? I want to know about her life, why she joined Skull Soul? Why did she want to die? I want to know her backstory, something terrible happened to her back before maybe" Nyleone said, "So you want to know about Kylie? Okay, I will try to find" Rie said,1 hour later, "Yes! Nyleone I have found it!" Rie said, "Oh! Can you tell me" Nyleone said, "Sure!" Rie said, "Kylie Johaan was a citizen of Jeksoda!" Rie said, "What? She was a citizen of Jeksoda!? Does she mean... she died where she lived before?" Nyleone asked, Rie continued, "Yes! At first, she lived in Jeksoda with her parents, when she was 12-year-old, her house was caught on fire and because of that...her mother died, all were sad, and Kylie started to become depressed, she thought to become a firefighter, so that no one else in the future could die like her mother, but she got 'Pyrophobia' (Fear of Fire), she started to hate campfires, bonfires, and lit candles, Kylie knew she wouldn't be able to become a firefighter like that, but she studied and applied for firefighter also! But, because she was always depressed so she wouldn't eat enough, she became weak, she was rejected in the application for not good health. She thought to get jobs in other fields but all rejected her, some for looks, some for health. She didn't know what to do. Also, she lived with her father! She thought that it would be nice to get a job in Hedwan, so she told her father about it, her father agreed, so she went to Hedwan but on the way, she was crying, "My poor dad... I am getting a job for you! You are 47-year-old. What will you do at this age, your daughter will do anything for you! But... your daughter can't do anything, not even getting a job! If I earn money then I could buy many things for us, food, clothes' ' She said and sobbed, "I need some money... How will I get money? I am also not getting any jobs," she thought. Suddenly someone pulled her, it was Mr. Dean, and from there she knew about Mr. Dean, because of money, she joined the gang. After joining the gang, she always thought about her father. A month later, he asked her friends, "I want to see my father! " Did anything happen to my father!?" Kylie asked, her friends did research and found out a message from Jeksoda News, 'Many people are dying in Hedwan but, A 47-year-old man also had died in Jeksoda! He have died from a very strange and unknown disease. Scientists, doctors are finding the disease....' Kylie was shocked and started to cry, "NO! Not father also..." she said, her friends comforted her, "Don't cry Kylie, be brave!" Cherylynne said. After her parents died, she also wanted to die, that's why she told you to kill her. And at the age of 20, she died by collapsing buildings. May Kylie and her parents rest in peace" Rie ended, "Oh... it's a very tragic story. May Johaan family rest in peace..." Nyleone prayed, "Thank you Rie! For finding the story about Kylie," Nyleone said, "Welcome, friend!" Rie replied and Nyleone went from Rie's house.

CHAPTER TWELVE

King Cyrus and Queen Rosa

FBI called Mr. Dean to the FBI office to ask questions,

"So, Mr. Dean, you are here to answer some of our questions. Do you understand?" The FBI asked, "Yes" Mr. Dean said, "Is Mr. Dean is your real name? If no, then what is your name?" They asked, "No, it is not my real name and my real name is Ben Speilberg," Mr. Dean said, "Ben Speilberg? Wait, is this Prince Ben!" A crew member said, "Yes!..... What!?.........

Prince Ben was the boss of the gang!?" The FBI's were shocked and confused, "Prince Ben, why have you made the gang?" The FBI asked, "You all know..." Prince Ben said, "No, we don't know, tell us!" The FBI said to Ben "Fine! I was the prince of Hedwan and the only son of King Victor. The year 2014, when I was 14-year-old, I went to explore Hedwan, after exploring, I went back to the Kingdom. Father told me, "Son, you should not become friends with the citizen, we should not talk to them also!" "But why, father?" I asked, "It is a long story... the citizens did very bad to your grandfather," Father said, "What?" I replied, "Long ago... It was the time of your grandfather, King Cyrus. He married Queen Rosa, your grandmother.

Mother was the most beautiful woman in Hedwan, and many people started to meet her, daily crowds were increasing, she hated crowds, so she told everyone to not meet her every day, all thought that the queen hate them, "Queen hates us! She doesn't want to meet us!" Everybody said, everyone the opposite of what Mother wanted, "Now, everyone hates me! I just wanted that not to crowd the place, and not to meet me every day, once in a week, but they thought the opposite! I don't want to show my face to the citizen, I will not meet them!" Mother said to Father, Father was confused about what to do, he thought to tell this to the citizen, King said "Citizens! Queen does not hate you all, she hates crowds-" "Just say that she hates us!" someone said, "Please listen to my full sentence!" Father said, "NO! WE WILL NOT!! QUEEN HATES US!!"All said, and father went away, for some days, father didn't meet the citizens, as he was depressed, "What can I do? The citizens are offended by us... 'Queen hates us' I hear it every time, 'because queen hates us, we hate her'... citizens have misunderstood but they are not listening to us... what should I do? " Father thought, and because of not meeting for many days, citizens thought that Father also hates them! When Father and Mother went to meet the citizens a month later, they saw hate! And they went inside as fast as they could, 'KING AND QUEEN HATE US!!' they just heard this... And they stopped meeting citizens, if they have to give any instructions, they will give those instructions to their ministers and the minister will say it to the citizens... a few years later, Father and Mother thought to meet the citizens, thinking they understood and forgot everything but... when they came to the stage, a few minutes later, someone sniped the father! Mother went inside, after knowing father died, mother became very sad, "Find who has killed him!" Mother said and after a few days, the sniper was caught, he was sentenced to death for killing the king, "Why did he kill the king?" Mother asked, "The citizens told him to do, 'King and Queen isn't worthy to become the king and queen! Kill them!' That's why he killed the king, he also wanted to kill you but you went inside" Mother was shocked and started to hate them, this hate was real! I was only 3-year-old that time. When I became 13-year-old, my mother told me the harsh truth about Hedwan's citizens. She also felt that maybe at some point it can be her mistake also...

CHAPTER THIRTEEN

Creating the Gang

Mother also told me to make a promise, "Promise that you will never meet the citizens! You also pass these words to your next generations!" she said, it became a tradition, we should never talk or meet our citizens, we can't break your grandmother's promise also! If you break, then you will be dethroned!" My father told me, Ben ended his grandparents' story. "How is this related to you making a gang?" The FBI asked, "People have forgotten everything, it's no use of hiding in the kingdom... I wanted to meet the citizens, I wanted to talk to them but Father didn't allow me. When I became 20-years-old, I became the new King of Hedwan, everything was fine until...one time, I met one citizen and talked to him, when father knew it, he dethroned me. I told my father that everyone has forgotten that situation, but he said, 'it's a tradition.' I didn't care. I remembered, when I was a kid, my father told me the power of being a king, I became greedy and wanted back that power, but I can't become king again... the only way to become king again was to kill my father!" Ben said. The FBI was shocked, "You wanted to kill the king!?" they asked. Ben continued, "So I went somewhere and was blabbing about how I will kill my father, but Oliver Sebastian, Father of Nyleone and a soldier in our kingdom was following me, he recorded what I was saying and sent it to his daughter, Nyleone. When I realized he was following me, I grabbed him, "You were following me?" and took his phone, I told him to call his daughter, he called, "Your father is with me! If you publish that record then I will kill your entire family!" Of course, after listening to that threat she didn't do anything with that record. I also started to live somewhere else, not in the kingdom. A week later, as normal, I switched on my television and saw the news, "Prince Ben planned to kill his father!" and the record started to play, and then many people said bad things to me,

'Prince Ben should be killed!' 'How can he think like that?' everyone said, and like my grandparents, I started to hate the citizens of Hedwan. At night, I called some of the ministers for help, "Bring some gangsters!" They brought, and I told them to kill the people who were in the news! Who told bad things about me!" The gangsters did as I said, my minsters gave them money, and I thought about killing everyone in the Hedwan because everyone hates me! I thought about forming a gang, with the ministers' money, I was able to buy two buildings and the necessary things for my gang. My ministers brought many gangsters and jobless people, and they became a member of my gang. Every day, someone dies. The FBI, police, all started to discover, how it is happening. More than 1000 people died in a year. I completely forgot about the Sebastian Family, I told my gang to kill the Sebastian Family, and a member killed Nyleone's father. I also needed more members. I had 1050 members, so I went outside to find some people. I saw a woman, it was Kylie! I told her to kill the Sebastian Sisters, she did but was not able to kill the eldest sister, Nyleone. Kylie also became a member of my gang. I also knew that Maria told her mother to go to her village so

I was not able to kill her. Some of my members told me the name of the gang, and they thought 'Skull Soul'. It was the story of last year, Kylie has not joined the gang, one member made the logo and badges for everyone so that we can know that the person is our member. One time, some of my members went to kill a person, by mistake, one person dropped his badge, the next day, a girl found it and gave it to the police, in that badge, it was written Skull Soul, like that, The Hedwan knew our gang's name. We had to change the badge's design because Hedwan knew about the badge's design and they could wear it and come to our headquarters if they knew our base's location. I also needed Nyleone so I told my gang to kidnap her, I needed Nyleone because I needed one person from the FBI, who can tell every move of the FBI but she refused to join my gang and escaped from my base. The FBI also knew my base's location so we have to shift somewhere but the FBI found it also, and all my members died, my properties are also destroyed." Ben ended the story. The FBI took him back to his cell...

King Cyrus also announced that Hedwan will become a democratic place, and Monarchy will stop! So, elections started. Nyleone's mother also came back from the village, and Nyleone and her mother started to live together. Everyone lived happily.

{THE END}

Kylie Johaan- wanted to get a job so she could earn money and make her father happy. Member of Skull Soul

Nyleone Sebastian- A FBI agent and wanted to find her sisters' murderer and to find information about the gang 'Skull Soul'

Sharon Sebastian- Sister of Nyleone

Maria Sebastian- Sister of Nyleone

Rie Bach- A FBI agent and friend of Nyleone

Ben Speilberg (Mr. Dean)- Was the prince and the boss of the gang, Skull Soul

Cherylynne Parks- Member of Skull Soul and friend of Kylie

Willam Jordon- Member of Skull Soul

Serena Woods- Member of Skull Soul

Stanley Woolf- Member of Skull Soul

Diana Curie- The spy of Skull Soul

Rose Luther- Friend of Sharon

Benjamin Bach- Rie's stepfather. He adopted Rie

Aiden Schumacher- The spy of Skull Soul and best friend of Diana

King Victor- Ben's Father

King Cyrus- Ben's Grandfather

Queen Rosa- Ben's Grandmother

Places Mentioned In The Story

(They all are fiction places, none of them are related to real-life)

Hedwan- Many murders were happening in this place

    Jeksoda- The place where Skull Soul shifted from their old one to a new base. Kylie's old house location

    Losia Medran Forest- Skull Soul's old base

    Mikin- Place where Rie lived, her old house's location